Original title:
Eccentric Ellipses

Copyright © 2025 Creative Arts Management OÜ
All rights reserved.

Author: Seraphina Caldwell
ISBN HARDBACK: 978-1-80567-867-0
ISBN PAPERBACK: 978-1-80567-988-2

The Uncommon Loop

In a world where circles frown,
A twisty line takes the crown.
It hops and skips, a jolly dance,
Chasing odd shapes, it takes a chance.

With knees bent high, it spins about,
Whispers secrets, sings out loud.
Bending reason in silly ways,
It bursts with laughter, brightening days.

Wandering Waves

Waves ripple through a field of dreams,
Wobbling left, then bursting at the seams.
Like jumpy jelly on the run,
Chasing shadows, seeking fun.

They tumble, giggle, slip and slide,
In this world, there's nothing to hide.
Each swish and sway, a playful tease,
Floating freely, like a breeze.

Flamboyant Curvatures

Curvy lines in colors bold,
Strike a pose, they're uncontrolled.
They waltz through skies of purple hues,
Dizzying all with bright blues clues.

They sprinkle joy from every bend,
A carnival where straight lines end.
Flaunting flair with every turn,
In this dance, there's much to learn.

Jests of Geometry

Shapes collide with comical flair,
Triangles giggle, unaware.
Squares throw pies, round ones retreat,
Laughter echoes, oh what a feat!

Pentagons jive, while hexagons sway,
Juggling angles in a delightful display.
Polygons play their quirky roles,
In this land of geometric goals.

Veils of the Unusual

In a world where the spoons wear hats,
And the cats throw dance parties in spats.
Umbrellas bloom from the ground in delight,
While fish on bicycles take off in flight.

Giraffes on stilts tickle the sky,
As penguins attempt to learn how to fly.
With sandwiches singing a merry tune,
Life spins like a merry-go-round in June.

Whimsies in Motion

Kites made of candy soar high with glee,
While frogs in top hats sip tea by the sea.
A clock that runs backward, oh what a sight,
Says, 'Stop wasting time, let's party tonight!'

Jumping jellies waltz across the floor,
As corndogs join in, 'Hey, let's explore!'
Every sprout dons a colorful coat,
And the daisies out sing the goats on a boat.

Loops of the Unseen

In the corner, a squirrel juggles some nuts,
While raccoons in pajamas give party cuts.
Tiny elephants shuffle with flair,
As music spills out from everywhere.

A pizza that dances on top of a truck,
Spins in the sunlight, oh what a luck!
With cupcakes on pogo sticks bouncing so proud,
Even the shadows burst out loud!

Deviations of Delight

Chickens in tutus do pirouettes bright,
As mouses hum tunes under soft moonlight.
A rainbow of socks in a fishbowl spins,
While the soup sings a song where the laughter begins.

Balloons made of cheese drift up in the air,
While toasters play games without a care.
With laughter that echoes and tickles the day,
In this land of silliness, we all want to stay.

Dreamy Revolutions

In circles we dance, not quite a square,
A jumpy little jig, with hardly a care.
Round and round, we spin like tops,
Each misstep a giggle, before the beat drops.

With wild ideas that float like balloons,
Chasing laughter beneath the bright moons.
Twists and turns in a silly parade,
A world full of dreams, where whimsy is made.

Quirky Constellations

Stars that wobble, and comets that shine,
In a sky that just giggles, all out of line.
Cacti wearing hats, oh what a sight,
Lighting up the cosmos, with pure delight.

Planets that wobble, like jello on plates,
Dance with the sun while the universe waits.
Galaxies toss confetti in glee,
As we laugh with the stars, endlessly free.

Irregular Harmonies

Tunes that skip and hop like a frog,
Blending notes that surprise like a fog.
A chorus of giggles in an offbeat bazaar,
Where laughter and music go bizarre.

Layers of whimsy, a pie out of place,
Melodies twist like a wild embrace.
Dancing along on the musical breeze,
Singing in laughter, just aim to please.

Playful Pathways

On crooked roads where chickens roam,
We follow the paths that feel like home.
Sidewalks twist like a curly fry,
Leading to laughter, oh me, oh my!

Signs that point to nowhere at all,
Amusing encounters where giggles enthrall.
With each step a bounce, and each turn a cheer,
Adventures await, bringing joy near.

Fancies in Flight

A chicken did a somersault,
In search of dreams most round and small.
It soared above the cotton clouds,
In polka dots, it danced and bowed.

A cow in shades of purple hue,
Sipped tea with hats of vibrant blue.
They laughed at flies who tried to soar,
And painted stripes on every door.

Orbital Oddities

A cat once tried to touch the moon,
With laces tied to a big balloon.
It swung around in tightest arcs,
And landed softly in the parks.

A hat grew legs and ran away,
Chased by socks on holiday.
They frolicked round the garden fair,
Creating shadows everywhere.

The Looping Lore

A shoe with jokes began to tell,
Of dancing fish that jumped so well.
They flopped and flipped in gooey streams,
Reviving childhood, full of dreams.

A spoon that twirled with endless grace,
Dined on cheese in an old suitcase.
It sang to forks of silver sheen,
In kitchens where the fairies gleam.

Strangely Shaped Echoes

A bubble bounced on sidewalk cracks,
With silly sounds and laughter hacks.
It giggled 'neath the bright sun's glow,
And sparked delight wherever it'd go.

A pencil drew a magic line,
Creating curves that felt divine.
It danced with paper, ink, and cheer,
As scribbles turned to dreams sincere.

Topsy-Turvy Tales

In a land where socks do dance,
And spoons hold a daring prance,
Teapots sing in joyful glee,
While chairs weave tales of jubilee.

The sun wears pants, a sight so rare,
Clouds throw parties in the air,
Cats paint stripes on every wall,
As laughter echoes, a free-for-all.

The Elusive Loop

Around and around, the rabbit flies,
Chasing its tail under pastel skies,
Wobbling fences, a laughable sight,
Where shadows giggle with pure delight.

Lollipops grow on bending trees,
Tickled by whispers from the breeze,
Cakes play hide-and-seek with the night,
As owls wear glasses, oh what a sight!

Whirlwind Whimsy

A fish in a tuxedo steals the show,
While jellybeans dance in a vibrant glow,
Balloons are kings of the open sky,
As quirky creatures all flutter by.

The clock ticks backward with a grin,
Time does tricks and jumps right in,
Where smiles tumble and frogs wear hats,
In this topsy-turvy world of chats.

Elusive Arcana

Octopuses juggle in the moonlight,
Spinning yarns of a fanciful flight,
Chocolates rain from a dainty tree,
As wacky gnomes all laugh with glee.

Mysteries hide in a candy jar,
Where dreams take off in a comical car,
The night plays games with a cheesy grin,
In a world where nonsense doth begin.

Wavy Narratives

In a world where fish fly high,
And cows wear hats that make them sigh,
A toaster danced a jolly jig,
While a cat recited poetry big.

Each sofa sprouted legs and ran,
Chasing after a marching band;
The clocks ticked backward, time unspun,
As teacups giggled just for fun.

A pancake painted on the wall,
As curtains sang a merry call,
A shoe-shaped car zoomed past me,
With passengers sipping honey tea.

And as the sun began to swirl,
The mushrooms twirled, a crazy whirl;
In this realm, laughter's the trend,
Where nonsense and joy blend at the end.

Convoluted Capers

A pickle wore a cape and flew,
While jellybeans played hopscotch too;
A spoon began to serenade,
As noodles lounged in sunshine laid.

On rollerblades, a salad zoomed,
Embracing chaos, never doomed;
The lemon danced with joy so bright,
While potatoes spun with sheer delight.

A walrus ran a lemonade stand,
While ants did acrobatics grand;
A feather floated free and wild,
In this silly world, we both smiled.

Juggling socks and juggling grins,
Unruly chaos always wins;
With laughter ringing in the air,
In convoluted capers, we share.

Joys of the Jumble

A bicycle sang a breezy tune,
Under the watch of a friendly moon;
A cookie climbed a leafy tree,
While squirrels debated infinity.

The fish wore glasses, reading books,
While muffins traded winks and looks;
A clock with legs ran round the park,
Chasing shadows until it's dark.

In this jumble of cheerful fun,
A hat on a hedgehog started to run;
A dancing broom swept up the beat,
As giggles echoed down the street.

With jelly on a trampoline,
And marshmallows wearing shades so keen,
The joys unfolded, twist and twirl,
In this whimsical, wondrous world.

Whirls of the Unexpected

In a world where spoons can dance,
And shadows sing in silly prance,
Kites wear glasses, twirl and leap,
While sleepy clouds begin to sleep.

Cats on bicycles zoom with glee,
Telling tales of wild decree.
With every twist and silly turn,
We find the joy, the lessons learn.

Cookies wearing hats so tall,
Join the party, come one, come all.
Giggles echo, laughter flows,
In this land where whimsy grows.

So let us ride this merry spree,
On roller skates made out of cheese.
For every chuckle and jolly shout,
Is a treasure we can't live without.

Asymmetrical Journeys

A turtle flies, a snail can sprint,
On journeys without a single hint.
Paths that twist like licorice ropes,
With every step, we'll build our hopes.

Hopping frogs in tuxedos strut,
With floppy hats, they dance and cut.
Balloons that giggle, hats that squeak,
In this odd place, fun's what we seek.

We surf on waves of jelly beans,
And sail on boats made out of dreams.
With wobbly charts and maps awry,
We find the odd, we laugh and fly.

So join us friends, let's take a ride,
On wiggly tracks where we collide.
With smiles that stretch from ear to ear,
In this quirky land, we shall not fear.

Chasing Curves

There's a raccoon dressed in a cape,
He leaps through hoops of silly shape.
Round and round his antics spin,
In laughter's chase, we all dive in.

Socks that dance and hats that sing,
Curvy lines are quite the thing.
With rubber ducks on roller skates,
Each twist and turn exhilarates.

Chasing circles, never straight,
In this world, we celebrate.
Giggling squirrels and tiny mice,
Join the fun, oh what a slice!

So let's embrace the winding road,
Where silly tales are freely flowed.
In every curve, a joy we find,
With laughter's echo, hearts entwined.

The Unusual Tangle

A spaghetti monster ties its shoes,
While jellybeans share the news.
With tangled hair and lopsided shoes,
We giggle at the silly views.

Puppies zoom with rainbow tails,
In boats made out of paper sails.
While quirky birds write comic strips,
And dance along with cheerful quips.

In this maze of cheerful clips,
Every twist brings smiles and flips.
With giggling trees that sway and sway,
We laugh together, come what may.

So join the fun and lose control,
In this delightful, wiggly stroll.
For in the odd, the fun's inherent,
In every tangle, hearts are fervent.

Wandering Degrees

In a land where angles play,
Squirrels dance the night away,
Triangles giggle in the sun,
While circles race, oh what fun!

Lines wobbly, full of grace,
Twist and turn, a wild chase,
Graphs do cartwheels, slack and free,
Numbers skipping, just like me!

Boundless Curvatures

A spiral staircase leads to bliss,
With banana-shaped paths, can't miss,
Cacti wear hats, oh what a sight,
As piñatas tumble day and night!

Bouncing angles, round they go,
Dancing pixies, stealing show,
Curves that giggle, teasing fate,
In this world, we celebrate!

Curves of Curiosity

Wiggly lines with puzzled hues,
Chasing puzzles, picking clues,
Doughnuts soar, and cheese does roll,
In this circus, we lose control!

Balloons that twist in wavy cheer,
Echoing laughter, loud and clear,
Carousels spin with a quirky ring,
Every turn, a wacky fling!

Whimsical Orbits

Planets sporting hats that twirl,
Gliding ducks in a cosmic whirl,
Stars that giggle, shine so bright,
As moons perform a silly fight!

Galaxies wrapped in cotton sweet,
Taking tumbles on their feet,
Silly comets laugh and tease,
In space, it's all just meant to please!

Flights of Curious Dreams

In a sky where penguins glide,
Balloons bounce with prancing pride.
Jellybeans wear little hats,
And dandelions throw tiny chats.

A cat sits high on purple wheels,
Sipping soup with clacking heels.
Rubber ducks race down the lane,
Chasing sunbeams, never plain.

Giraffes play hopscotch in the night,
While fireflies flash with sheer delight.
Tacos dance in their own parade,
While moonbeams sing a serenade.

And in this world, my heart takes flight,
Where dreams are strange, and smiles are bright.
So here's to laughs in every scheme,
In this land of curious dreams!

The Uncharted Arc

A llama dons a pirate hat,
While squirrels chat with a tipple of chat.
Wombats offer tea and toast,
While fish take flight, they love it most.

Flying saucers zoom and twirl,
As fashion shows with cats unfurl.
Jelly jars on bicycles race,
With giggles bouncing in every space.

A walrus juggles wobbly pies,
While frogs play chess beneath the skies.
Unicorns wear socks of plaid,
In this arc, it's just a fad.

With giggles and grins, we roam about,
In silly lands where joy's the route.
So grab your friend and take a whirl,
In the arc where quirkiness twirls!

Peculiar Pathways

Down a path where bubbles sing,
And flowers wear a slinky ring.
A snail plays drums upon a shell,
As toothpaste rivers bid farewell.

Kites made from waffles fly so high,
While pigs on skateboards zoom and sigh.
Pickles dance in flamingo shoes,
And everyone shares their silly views.

Raccoons in capes lead the way,
Through a forest where giggles play.
Marshmallow clouds drift in laughter,
In this journey, joy's the thereafter.

So let us skip on this odd trail,
With every whim and every tale.
For quirky steps bring a light heart,
As we wander where laughter starts!

Enigmatic Circles

In circles drawn by crayons bright,
Bunnies do the waltz at night.
Hats that spin and shoes that squeak,
In this world, it's laughs we seek.

Ovens bake with giggling pies,
While trains of candy zoom and rise.
A dance of spoons sways here and there,
As cupcakes toss their frosted hair.

A fish in glasses reads the news,
While turtles strut in polka-dots, too.
And somewhere near a tree so tall,
A clever squirrel plans a ball.

So come and join this jolly show,
Where every circle's bound to glow.
With laughter and smiles, let's all embark,
In this whimsical, enigmatic park!

Circling Secrets

Round and round the puzzle spins,
Whispers dance where laughter begins.
Hidden tales in every twirl,
Giggles bubble as secrets unfurl.

In a loop, the questions chase,
Fanciful thoughts go every place.
Who can guess the next big twist?
Catch a wink, you might have missed!

Chasing clues like kids at play,
In this game, we lose our way.
But with every spin, we find,
A joyfully tangled state of mind.

Oh, the fun of silly spins,
While time eludes, our laughter wins.
With twists and turns, we'll always seek,
The merry secrets that we peek!

A Mosaic of Movements

Colors blend in quirky ways,
Each twist and turn, brightens our days.
A patchwork of laughter in every stride,
With bold eruptions that collide.

Funky dances break the norm,
While giggles gather, a happy swarm.
Every step a playful tease,
As we waltz with giddy knees.

Shapes that wobble and sway about,
In this jigsaw of joy, there's no doubt.
Every motion sings a tune,
That sends our spirits up to the moon!

We waddle, we jiggle, oh what a sight,
Creating laughter, pure delight.
Each moment unexpected and bright,
In this mosaic, we feel so light!

Eccentric Arcs

Curves that giggle, bends that cheer,
Wobbly paths draw us near.
We take a leap, then we glide,
Finding joy on this quirky ride.

Swirling spirals, life's delight,
Bouncing high, feeling light.
With every arc, we laugh out loud,
A circus of thoughts, well-rounded and proud.

Skirting corners, we jump with glee,
Hilarious draws, wild and free.
Twists and twirls in zany jest,
A rollercoaster of fun, the very best!

With silly paths, we play the fool,
In the geometry of laugh, we rule.
We embrace the wobbly spree,
In every arc, pure jubilee!

Surreal Curves

Curly cues of misfit dreams,
Where nothing's ever as it seems.
Bizarre shapes splashed with glee,
Who thought this could ever be?

With wiggles, jigs, and jests galore,
We weave together, asking for more.
Reality bends, smiles collide,
In a landscape where fun resides.

Silly structures in vibrant hues,
Peculiar paths that amuse and confuse.
Every curve, a new surprise,
Filling our hearts with comic highs!

So let us swirl in quirky delight,
To dance with shadows in broad daylight.
For in this surreal, playful maze,
We find our joy in the silliest ways!

Enigmatic Ellipses

In circles strange, we twirl and spin,
With laughter ringing, let the games begin.
A hop, a skip, around we go,
In our own world, with tales to sow.

A wobbly dance, our feet askew,
Chasing shadows, just me and you.
We wear mismatched socks, a comical sight,
In this quirky realm, we take flight.

We build our forts with pillows and glee,
Pretend to sail on a vast, blue sea.
Our thoughts bounce like rubber in the air,
With giggles and quirks, we make our share.

Oh, what a ride, this bizarre parade,
Where silly dreams and plans are made.
Let's toss confetti and dance in delight,
In our madcap world, it feels just right.

Offbeat Odes

With hats askew and shoes untied,
Off we wander, side by side.
Our songs are silly, our steps a prank,
In this curious land, we dance and clank.

Strange little critters join the ride,
On roller skates, they glide and slide.
Down the lane, we sing and shout,
As laughter spills, there's no doubt.

We tiptoe through puddles, splashy and wild,
In the realm of the wacky, we're all just a child.
Kites made of dreams twirl up to the sky,
With goofy grins, we let them fly.

Our odes are woven in random delight,
In the glow of the stars and the soft moonlight.
Together we laugh, beneath twinkling beams,
In our offbeat world, we chase our dreams.

Subtle Undulations

Waves of laughter, they rise and fall,
In this zany space, come one, come all.
We giggle like kids, with ice cream cones,
Where silliness blooms and mischief roams.

Bouncing around, on a trampoline wide,
Here, fun spills over, can't let it hide.
With silly faces and eyes that gleam,
We float through adventures, like a wild stream.

Each twist and turn, a wondrous surprise,
In a world of wonder, where happiness lies.
Kites soaring high like our hopes in the air,
With whimsy and grace, we dance without care.

Like ripples in water, our joy emanates,
Chasing the magic that laughter creates.
In these subtle shifts, where fun intertwines,
Let's embrace the quirky in life's designs.

The Wind's Whimsy

The breeze carries giggles, featherlight,
As we skip along, from morning to night.
With nature's grace, we twirl and sway,
In the playful rhythm of a carefree day.

A windy whisper, it tickles our ears,
Crafting wild stories, erasing our fears.
We chase paper boats down the streams of delight,
In the arms of the wind, everything's right.

Our sneakers dance on a canvas of green,
Where silliness reigns, a joyful scene.
Through rustling leaves and a tangle of hair,
In this whimsical world, there's magic to share.

So come take a ride with the breeze at your back,
On a journey of fun, no room for slack.
Life's an adventure, we're never quite tame,
In the wind's merry dance, we'll play our game.

Bouncing Between Realities

In a world that spins like a top,
Cats wear hats that somehow flop.
Fish in suits dance with flair,
While frogs in bowties float in air.

A toaster sings a tune at dawn,
Whispers secrets, then it's gone.
Chairs play chess, wise and sly,
While socks conspire with a pie.

We chase our shadows, giggling loud,
As bubbles form a wacky crowd.
Bananas slide down roller coasters,
And teapots race as manic roasters.

In dreams, we bounce from place to place,
With silly grins on every face.
Reality's just a jester's game,
Where nothing's quite the same again.

The Conundrum of Circles

Round and round, the wheels do spin,
While hamsters plot to sneak a win.
Bicycles wear some quirky hats,
And dance with over-enthused cats.

Triangles stare in disbelief,
As circles steal their comic relief.
A square attempts to walk a line,
But ends up looking so divine.

The sun plays tag with the moon's light,
While stars giggle at the sight.
Each twist and turn's a silly plight,
Where logic takes a charming flight.

In this odd world where shapes unite,
We marvel at the strange delight.
Cartwheeling in a daisy chain,
Frolicking in the summer rain.

Oddball Echoes

Whispers roll like bowling balls,
Hitchhiking through the hallowed halls.
A dancing broom, a groovy knight,
Spin tales of nonsense and delight.

Jellybeans wear polka dots,
While jellyfish and donuts plot.
They waltz around on giant feet,
As rainbows giggle, oh so sweet.

Echoes bounce off painted walls,
Ticklish giggles down the stalls.
A paradox in every sound,
Where sense and nonsense swirl around.

In a realm where laughter reigns,
Absurdity courses through our veins.
We sing a song that's out of tune,
With harmony that sways the moon.

Unpredictable Patterns

Stripes of chaos, dots of fun,
Jumpy rhythms on the run.
Socks might wear a plaid today,
While coats prance in a funky way.

Birds in blazes, pink on blue,
Chirp wildly like they've lost a clue.
Pants converse with sleeves galore,
In a tango, they hit the floor.

Raindrops twist into a jig,
While umbrellas laugh, fold, and dig.
They catch the wind, a mischievous gust,
In a swirl of joy and aimless trust.

Life's a dance of fit and fine,
With patterns that blur by design.
In whimsical bliss, we twirl and dive,
Where funny moments come alive.

Curves of Whimsy

In a land of loops so round,
A cat wore shoes, quite profound.
With hats that spun like tops on high,
He meowed a joke, then waved goodbye.

The flowers danced in wobbly hues,
While squirrels played in rainbow shoes.
A teapot sang a jazzy tune,
Beneath the shade of a purple moon.

Each tree had limbs that wiggled free,
A sight that made the bumblebees glee.
They spun and twirled on merry trails,
As laughter echoed in their sails.

The cows wore glasses and read the news,
While chickens jived to funky blues.
In this land, bizarre and bright,
Every day felt just like night.

Paths of Oddity

Beneath the sky, a spiral twist,
A penguin danced with a jellyfish.
They slid and glided without a care,
Creating chaos in midair.

The fish wore socks, the frogs wore ties,
While toast flew past with buttered skies.
A wizard sneezed, and off he went,
With swirling sparkles, he was bent.

A snail recited an epic rhyme,
While crickets cheered in perfect time.
Balloons floated in a wily race,
Each one a smile, a silly face.

The trees held hands, a quirky crew,
As apples sang a tune or two.
In this realm where fun ignites,
We chased our shadows through the nights.

Spirals of the Uncommon

A crooked road with no clear end,
Where rabbits hop and turtles bend.
With candy clouds that drip and swirl,
And gummy bears that twist and twirl.

The sun wore shades and cracked a grin,
As clouds played tag with a sly wind.
A clock tick-tocked in syncopation,
Counting giggles in celebration.

The shadows danced with spider feet,
In every corner, a funny beat.
A kite was stuck in a tree so tall,
It waved hello, then began to fall.

With laughter spilling from the skies,
And jellybeans that claimed to fly.
This wacky world, so strange and bright,
Turns every frown into delight.

The Dance of Quirky Orbits

Upon a path that loops around,
A mouse wore shoes that squeaked and bound.
It twirled in circles, spun with grace,
Chasing its tail in this funny space.

A bicycle flew past a dancing tree,
It whistled tunes like a melody.
The flowers chuckled, their petals wide,
As a toaster danced in the sunny tide.

The stars winked down, mischievous and bright,
While comets zipped, a humorous sight.
In this ballet of giggles and quirks,
Reality playfully jerks and lurks.

As moonbeams tickled the grassy ground,
Joyful echoes of laughter abound.
So round and round, we joyfully spin,
In a world where the fun begins.

Trails of the Offbeat

There once was a man with a shoe on his head,
He danced through the streets, just like the dead.
With a wink and a smile, he twirled like a kite,
A joyfully oddball, a curious sight.

His cat wore a hat, quite a sight to behold,
She strutted her stuff, oh so brave and so bold.
Together they laughed, against all the norms,
Creating their fun, in their own silly forms.

The Geometry of Surprises

In a world where squares tried to roll like a ball,
Came a triangle, laughing, and took quite a fall.
It whispered a joke to a circle so round,
And soon all the shapes were giggling unbound.

An octagon joined with a wink and a cheer,
Said, "Life's too short for dull angles, my dear!"
They danced in a way that defied simple rules,
Making math seem like fun, not just for the fools.

Riddles in the Round

A pizza was spinning, oh what a delight,
With toppings that danced, just perfect for a bite.
But one slice declared it preferred to fly,
So it zipped through the air, to the moon in the sky.

The crust gave a chuckle, 'You're leaving us flat!'
The cheese and the sauce said, 'Imagine that!'
But they knew quite well this would bring back their friend,
For round things get lost, but they always amend.

Bends of the Imagination

A noodle with dreams of becoming a snake,
Said, "I'll slither and giggle with each little shake!"
But while on his journey, he tripped on a spoon,
And giggled and squirmed to the light of the moon.

A muffin, so fluffy, with sprinkles galore,
Joined in the fun, what a wonderful score!
Together they danced through a whimsical night,
In a world spun from dreams, full of silly delight.

Twisted Journeys

On a path that zigzags wide,
A snail raced with a grinning ride.
Turning corners with silly flair,
It squeaked out loud, "I'm almost there!"

The trees all dance with laughter loud,
A squirrel wearing a tiny shroud.
Chasing shadows that bounce and flee,
Oh, what a sight! Just wait and see!

Sideways glances at bending signs,
A frog leaps high on fluffy lines.
Round and round in perfect glee,
What a wild, wobbly jamboree!

With each step, more giggles bloom,
As bumbles buzz in dizzy room.
They swirl and twirl in joyful fights,
Dancing freely through starry nights.

Whirling Fantasies

In a kettle that hops and spins,
Tea parties host mischievous twins.
They stir the brew with twirly straws,
And giggle loudly, raising applause!

Cupcakes roll on sugar hills,
Frosted dreams fulfill our thrills.
Marshmallow clouds drift on by,
Puffing joy in the sunny sky!

A rubber chicken plays the flute,
While penguins dance in feathered suits.
Bubbles bounce with a playful cheer,
As laughter rings from ear to ear!

Whirlwinds of fun spin round and round,
In a kingdom where jesters abound.
They juggle life with silly grace,
In this world, we laugh and race!

Doodles in Motion

A pencil rolls on bouncy tracks,
Sketching giggles and silly snacks.
Every line is a bounce and jig,
Painting laughter both large and big!

Displayed in colors, bright and bold,
A cat in a hat, oh, what a hold!
He prances around in mismatched shoes,
Twirling stories for us to choose.

Pies float by on wings of cream,
While dancing spoons chase a dream.
Each doodle spins a comic tale,
Of wobbling whales on tiny trails!

Laughter lives in each bright sweep,
In sketchy realms where sillies leap.
A world alive with playful fun,
Where doodles dance 'til day is done!

Spirited Spins

A whirlwind twirls with vibrant zest,
As paper hats go on a quest.
Twisting freely, they laugh and whine,
In a merry-go-round of sparkling wine!

Frogs on roller skates zoom past,
In races that just can't be outclassed.
Their laughter echoes through the air,
A chorus found in joyful flair!

Oh, to spin like a joyful leaf,
In a breeze of tickles and disbelief.
Round and round, the fun won't cease,
As party vibes bring sweet release!

Every spin is a spark of cheer,
Turning the mundane into a sphere.
So grab a friend and join the ride,
In spirited spins, let laughter glide!

Playgrounds of Precision

In the land where circles dream,
All the angles plot and scheme.
A ruler's laugh, a compass twist,
Mathematics thrown into the mist.

Count the swings that sway and churn,
Spin the slides, take a daring turn.
Jumping jacks that hop and skip,
Angles wobble, logic drips.

Chalky lines in vibrant hues,
Draw a box, but it's really shoes.
Shapes collide, a joyous clash,
Building towers made of trash.

In this space where shapes unite,
Even circles may take flight.
Giggles echo, numbers play,
In precision's fun display.

Harmonies in Hiccups

A hiccup here, a burp or two,
Round notes bouncing, isn't it true?
In quirky rhythms we shall sway,
A symphony that's gone astray.

Every giggle a musical note,
As our laughter begins to float.
Percussion made with claps and snaps,
Poetic slips in silly laps.

Catch a tune in the hiccup's breath,
Life's a laugh, no fear of death.
With a twist and a twirl we sing,
Join the tune, let joy take wing!

So let the hiccups guide your way,
In harmony, we shall play.
Each little sound a joyful quirk,
In this whirlwind we all smirk.

Gravity's Grin

Down we plunge in joyous glee,
Feeling light yet oddly free.
Round and round, the world spins fast,
Wobbling wonders can't be passed.

Up above, the balloons ascend,
In a dance of physics, we pretend.
Flying high and tugged by strings,
Playing chase like boisterous kings.

Noses pressed against the glass,
Watching as the seconds pass.
With a bounce, the ground does sway,
Oh, what fun in a silly way!

In every slip, in every dash,
Laughter echoes, hearts all thrash.
Gravity giggles, take the ride,
Join the whimsy, let joy guide.

The Flux of Fancies

In a world where oddities bloom,
Whimsical thoughts dispel the gloom.
Dancing thoughts in playful flight,
Capture dreams 'neath starlit night.

Wacky whims with colors bright,
Sprinkle laughter, chase the light.
In this realm where fancies soar,
Reality becomes a lore.

Juggling quirks from dusk till dawn,
Round and round, a colorful con.
Every thought a vibrant dance,
In the chaos, take a chance!

So spin your tales, let weirdness reign,
In the flux, we'll break the chain.
With a chuckle, spread your wings,
In the fancy realm, joy sings.

Spirited Spirals

In circles we spin, a merry dance,
Chasing our tails, not missing a chance.
With laughter that echoes, the joking begins,
Around and around, where nonsense wins.

A duck in a top hat, a cat on a swing,
Juggling bananas, oh what joy they bring!
Twists that confound, we giggle and sway,
In spirals of whimsy, we frolic and play.

Confetti and bubbles, a whirlwind of glee,
Pies in the face, oh what sight to see!
Chasing the laughter as it bounces along,
In a loop of delight, we all sing our song.

So come join the chaos, don't be left behind,
In spiraled mischief, let's see what we find.
With jokes up our sleeves and a sparkle so bright,
We'll twirl through the day and dance into night.

The Joy of Tangents

On paths that divert, we giggle with glee,
A plot twist of laughter, come journey with me.
Why walk in a straight line when curves can be fun?
Let's zigzag through weirdness until we are done.

A penguin in socks, doing a slide,
Cacti in tutus, what a strange ride!
With paths that diverge, we'll never be bored,
As long as we have our silly accord.

Sideways we dance, with a twist of the fate,
Underneath rainbow lights, we celebrate.
Skipping and hopping, we'll never be straight,
In a world full of curves, we're bound to create.

So grab a tall hat and a wobbly shoe,
Join in the laughter, let's make something new.
For tangents are funny, and laughter is free,
On the roads gone astray, we'll find jubilee.

Jigsaw Journeys

With pieces that float, let's see where we go,
A puzzle of laughter, a quirky tableau.
Each edge is a giggle, each corner a grin,
In a jigsaw of joy, where we all fit in.

A llama with glasses, an octopus rare,
A teapot on wheels zipping through the air!
We'll search for connections, and stitches of fun,
In this jigsaw of life, we'll get it done.

From chaos to order, we'll make our own game,
A world full of whimsy, never the same.
With each mismatched piece, the stories unfold,
In journeys of laughter, worth more than gold.

So gather your snippets, your silly old dreams,
In this jigsaw adventure, let's burst at the seams.
For together we'll giggle and craft something bright,
Each piece tells a story, a scene of delight.

Curls of Chaos

In curls that spiral, we twist and we turn,
With humor as fuel, there's much we can learn.
A noodle in socks, spaghetti for hair,
In the chaos of laughter, we find our own flair.

A turtle in slippers, with dance moves so slick,
A pizza that jokes, with a magic trick!
Wrapped in confusion, we tumble and roll,
In curls that entangle, we find our own soul.

From wiggles to giggles, let's splash and let loose,
In a world full of nonsense, we'll cut it all loose.
With whimsy our compass, let's wander and play,
In curls of hilarity, we'll brighten the day.

So come join the party, don't shiver or shake,
In curls of sweet chaos, we'll spin and we'll make.
With laughter as treasure, we'll ride the wild tides,
In giggles and joy, our bright spirit abides.

Twists of Fancy

In a world where cats ride bikes,
And penguins wear their Sunday spikes,
I found a frog who spilled some tea,
And laughed until I lost my key.

A chicken danced upon a log,
While turtles raced a nimble dog,
They twirled and spun in wild delight,
My heart was light, my face was bright.

The trees all wore their socks askew,
And squirrels grabbed a peanut brew,
With giggles echoing through the park,
As squirrels played the banjo, hark!

So join the fun, come take a ride,
On fanciful thoughts, let joy collide,
In this madcap land, oh what a spree,
Where laughter blooms like daisies free.

Unraveled Trajectories

A rocket blasted off on Monday,
But landed where the monkeys play,
They offered snacks of jelly beans,
And danced in circles, oh so keen.

The planets twirled in silly styles,
And winked at us with cosmic smiles,
A comet juggled with a star,
While astronauts played air guitar.

Each trajectory took a twist,
Where gravity ceased to exist,
They flipped and flopped in the great beyond,
Where logic and reason were fondly conned.

So let your mind just drift and sway,
In this absurd, delightful play,
For in the chaos, fun will reign,
In a universe so very strange.

Curved Confessions

A snail confessed to losing pace,
While mushrooms giggled, oh what grace,
They sprawled in shapes, a silly sight,
Under a disco ball so bright.

The beetles donned their bowler hats,
And waltzed with nearby chittering rats,
With each faux pas, they broke the rule,
Inventing dance in a chalkboard school.

With every curve, a secret shared,
A butterfly flared, boldly dared,
To leap and twirl in whimsy's grip,
A marvelous, mythical friendship trip.

So let us swirl in laughs galore,
As stories tumble and spirits soar,
In this land of twisty confessions,
Where joy is found in wild expressions.

The Nonsense of Movement

A bubble danced across the air,
With jellyfish that didn't care,
They floated high and wobbled wide,
While rubber ducks bounced side to side.

Fish played tag in a circular pond,
While thoughtless turtles waved and yawned,
The bees wore hats, the frogs made jokes,
As laughter burst from silly folks.

A whirlwind spun in colors bright,
And tickled those in its wild flight,
In clashes of wings and swirls of glee,
What chaos! Oh, how happy we'll be.

So come and join this merry spree,
Where nonsense reigns, and giggles flee,
For in this movement, pure delight,
We'll dance with shadows through the night.

The Quirk in the Curve

Round and round the tumbleweed,
A twisty dance that makes you plead.
In every bend, a giggle nested,
Life's silly paths are double-fested.

Curly-cues and wobbly lines,
Balancing on fragile signs.
A jump or skip, then a tumble,
Laughter echoes, never humble.

Swaying trees and hoppy clowns,
In this funny show, nobody frowns.
Each turn a chuckle, each spin a cheer,
As the world winks, nothing to fear.

Chasing goofballs down the lane,
Silly songs in minor rain.
In the quirk, we find our glee,
A merry chase, just you and me.

Lopsided Lullabies

Whimsical whispers float through the air,
Lopsided dreams with a quirky flair.
Off-kilter melodies dance in your head,
As stuffed bears sway in their cozy bed.

Banana peels slip beneath our feet,
While giggles and snorts make the night sweet.
Socks do a jig on the laundry line,
In this topsy-turvy world, oh how we shine!

The moon grins wide, its cheeks all aglow,
As stars trip and tumble in a goofy show.
Catch the laughter in the night sky,
With lopsided lullabies, let worries fly.

Glancing sideways, the shadow spins,
A crooked smile as the fun begins.
In the joy of awkward serenades,
We'll dance on dreams, and never fade!

Kaleidoscopic Chronicles

Through a prism of joy we take a peek,
Twisting tales in colors unique.
Jellybeans bouncing, a rainbow parade,
Each quirk a laugh, no worries made.

Storybooks drop their linear plots,
As we chase the whims of whimsical thoughts.
Glittery gnomes ride unicycles fast,
In this swirl of joy, we forget the past.

A polka-dotted anvil, a dancing shoe,
Each moment's a riddle, each giggle is new.
Cupcakes sing while the sun plays tag,
In kaleidoscopic dreams, no need to brag!

Colorful quirks, swirling delight,
As we weave our tales in the soft twilight.
Hold on to the giggles, let the colors flow,
In these chronicles, let our spirits glow.

Spheres of Surprise

Orbs of wonder roll down the lane,
Bouncing laughter, no room for pain.
Each sphere a riddle, each giggle a clue,
Find the fun in shapes anew.

Rolling marbles spill out their tales,
As we skip along, ignoring the scales.
Roundabout antics on sunny days,
Chasing delight in playful ways.

Juggling spoons and cups on a quest,
With loopty-loops and no time to rest.
In these spheres, surprises abound,
With hugs and chuckles all around.

Like rubber ducks in mismatched socks,
We discover joy, no need for locks.
In the whirl of laughter, the world seems bright,
With spheres of surprise, everything's right.

Kaleidoscope Daydreams

Colors spin and twist, oh what a sight,
Shadows play tricks in the fading light.
A cat in a hat rides a bicycle too,
While dancing on clouds with a purple kangaroo.

Rabbits juggle pencils in mid-air,
Chasing after whispers, it's quite the affair.
Rainbows dive into cups of tea,
As giggling trees sway in harmony.

A fish wearing glasses reads a book,
And a snail plays chess with a clever rook.
All in a world that's oh so bright,
Every moment a laugh, pure delight!

So join the fun in this dream so grand,
Where chuckles sprout from the ticklish sand.
With every blink, the absurd unfolds,
In kaleidoscope hues, laughter beholds.

Quizzical Circuits

Wires in wigs hum a cheerful tune,
While robots frolic like kids in June.
A toaster debates with a quirky lamp,
About the mysteries of a digital stamp.

Squirrels with gadgets are plotting a scheme,
To take over the park in a crazy dream.
They roll on wheels, with nuts to trade,
While coffee cups dance in a caffeinated parade.

The printer sneezes, ejecting confetti,
As a calendar does cartwheels, oh so petty!
They laugh and they twirl, in such silly ways,
In a world where nonsense is king of the days.

So plug in the laughter, let circuits unite,
For the quirkiest fun on this electric night.
With giggles and gadgets, let's spin and whirl,
In this zany realm where ideas unfurl.

Dancing Degrees

Curves waltz around in the warm summer air,
Spinning in patterns both unusual and rare.
A circle in polka dots, oh what a sight,
While triangles jiggle, so happy and bright.

Angles do tango on the marble floor,
As a square shimmies, then shouts out for more!
Gears groove together, practicing their steps,
In a nutshell dance, with no room for prep.

Each shape has a story, a laugh to unfold,
With pirouettes in a ballroom of gold.
A compass gets dizzy, but loves the thrill,
As curves glide past in a joyous chill.

So come join the shapes, let the music play,
In this rhythmic circle of wild display.
With every twist, the laughter grows,
In a world of geometry, where humor flows.

The Jester's Orbit

Up in the sky spins a comical sphere,
Full of a giggle, it's perfectly clear.
A jester rides planets with bells on his toes,
As stardust confetti from cosmic winds blows.

He juggles with meteors, spins them with grace,
While comets all dance in a joyous embrace.
Each flip and each grin brings a chuckle or cheer,
As laughter transcends through the vacuum of sphere.

With moons that wear hats and suns that blink bright,
He twirls with the stars, such a magical sight.
In this circus of orbits, the silliness flies,
Painting the cosmos with mirth-filled skies.

So gaze at the heavens, let giggles take flight,
Join the jester's party, oh what sheer delight!
In a universe where folly takes hold,
Laughter's the treasure, more precious than gold.

Tidal Twists

A fish in a hat, swimming with glee,
Waves doing the cha-cha, oh can't you see?
They flip and they flop in a jolly parade,
With bubbles a-bursting, a splashy charade.

Seagulls in tuxedos, what a fine sight,
Squawking their jokes through the day and the night.
They'll dance on the waves, spin and twirl,
While crabs in a conga delight in a whirl.

Clams play the drums on the shells that they wear,
Beaming with joy, with ocean to spare.
They shimmy and shake, it's a party on sand,
With tides pulling laughter, oh isn't it grand?

So come on, let's sway, let the currents bend,
With winks from the sea, where the fun never ends.
The ocean's a jester, in frolic and spritz,
Giggling at all of these tidal twists.

Fragmented Fragments

A puzzle of giggles snapped out of line,
Each piece is a riddle, quite quirky, divine.
Noses like squids and shoes shaped like cakes,
Amongst all the people, the laughter still quakes.

Toasters play chess with the bees in the park,
While socks tell tall tales until way after dark.
With wobbly tables that dance on their feet,
And pancakes that flip like a high-flying feat.

A donut with glasses maneuvers the scene,
While apples do ballet, so goofy and keen.
They twirl through the air with a wink and a smile,
In this world of fragments, absurdity's style.

So gather those pieces, don't lose track of mirth,
In smiles and in giggles, we find our true worth.
An orchestra of nonsense, a grand little act,
In the land of the silly, joy's never abstract.

Chasing Shadows

There's a cat with a hat, prancing in sun,
Chasing shadows around, oh what goofy fun!
With twirls and with leaps, it winks at the breeze,
Demanding attention and giggling with ease.

A dog on a skateboard, what a sight to behold,
Riding with style, yet never too bold.
As shadows take shape, they start to perform,
In a circus of whimsy, a cartoonish norm.

Pigeons are diving with grace and with flair,
Dressed up in top hats, without a care.
They taunt and they tease, as they fly in a row,
Playing tag with the shadows that swish to and fro.

So let's join the chase, with no need for a plan,
In the company of whimsy, we'll utterly span.
With laughter leading our whimsical flight,
Chasing shadows of humor until the night.

Looping Laughter

In a town where the clocks tick backward and spin,
A chicken in sneakers is ready to win.
With giggles a-plenty, it dances a jig,
On a loop of pure joy, it's all very big.

Jump ropes made of gummy, a candy delight,
As cats in the moonlight put up quite a fright.
They flip and they flop, in a dizzying spree,
With magic in motion, what fun it can be!

The trees wear pajamas, quite dapper and cute,
As they sway and they sway, in their jolly tall suit.
The world's such a circus, with laughter unfurled,
As we loop like a ribbon around this wild world.

So come gather 'round, let's giggle and cheer,
In this endless loop of delightful good cheer.
With hearts wide and carefree, let's revel and play,
In a whirlwind of laughter, forever to stay.

Odd Angles of Affection

In a world that bends and weaves,
Laughter spins as heart perceives.
A crooked smile, a tilted grin,
Love's geometry makes us spin.

Wobbly paths we stroll along,
Singing out our silly song.
With hearts askew, we dance a jig,
In odd-shaped joy, we continue big.

With every twist, a chuckle flows,
As angles change, our humor grows.
Each glance a twist of fate's design,
In quirky love, we're quite divine.

So gather round, embrace the strange,
For passion's quirks will never change.
Embrace the fun, the odd, the sweet,
In love's odd angles, life's complete.

Meandering Melodies

A tune that dances off the page,
With merry notes that laugh and rage.
Each pitch a loop, a swirl, a spin,
In harmony where quirks begin.

The rhythm skips like a bouncing ball,
In melodies that tease and thrall.
A reeling song, a playful fling,
As crazy chords our spirits bring.

From flutes that wobble to drums that roll,
Each sound a giggle that fills the soul.
A symphony of whims and dreams,
With quizzical notes that burst at seams.

So hum along, let laughter soar,
In whimsical tunes, we can't ignore.
Our hearts entwined in silly play,
In meandering joy, we find our way.

Chaotic Harmony

In tangled tunes where laughter thrives,
A chorus sings of wacky lives.
Each note a tumble, a playful tease,
In chaos found, we find our ease.

With rhythms that collide and clash,
We dance and laugh in goofy mash.
Off-kilter beats make spirits rise,
With every stumble, more surprise.

A jumbled mix of hearts and sound,
In this sweet chaos, love is found.
We twirl and spin with joyous glee,
In perfect chaos, we are free.

So let the tunes be wild and loud,
Embrace the crazy, wear it proud.
In harmony's most joyful strife,
We find the wackiness of life.

Roundabout Reflections

In circles spun with gleeful turns,
Life's dizzy dance, our passion burns.
Mirrored laughs, we gaze and see,
The quirky traits of you and me.

Around we go, a playful chase,
In swirling paths, we find our place.
Each joyful loop a journey unfolds,
In roundabout ways, our story told.

With every spin, a chuckle shared,
In silly ways, how much we've dared.
We weave through twists, embrace the odd,
In merry circles, we applaud.

So take my hand, let's spin some more,
In odd reflections, joy we explore.
With laughter bright as skies above,
In roundabout ways, we find our love.

Spirals of Serenity

In a world that looks askew,
Marbles roll with nothing new.
Cats in hats pursue their tails,
As laughter dances, joy prevails.

Twists and turns in every step,
A penguin waltzes, what a prep!
With frogs in boots and fish in ties,
It's a jolly world, oh how it flies!

Jelly beans in sapling trees,
Sailboats race on warm, sweet breeze.
Stars wear glasses, quite bemused,
As the moon juggles, unexcused.

So let's rejoice in this delight,
Where nonsense gives the world its light.
Embrace the quirks that make us grin,
In spirals, life is where we win!

The Dance of Offbeat Cycles

Bicycles with one big wheel,
Dance to a funny, quirky reel.
Marshmallows jump on pogo sticks,
While lizards wear their fancy picks.

Round and round, they twirl and spin,
As sing-song voices swell within.
A monkey leads a conga line,
While pickles prance, and lemons shine.

In this wild and wacky show,
Daisies wear the finest glow.
With cupcakes moving side to side,
We chuckle at the joy they hide.

So join the dance, don't miss your fate,
Where all things silly oscillate.
With offbeat rhythms, let's take chance,
In this peculiar, jovial dance!

Erratic Paths of Dreams

On paths where jelly beans do grow,
And all the dandelions glow.
A unicorn on roller skates,
Twists and turns that fate creates.

The clouds sip tea and share a joke,
While surfboards glide, with playful smoke.
Kites with shoes, they soar and dive,
In whimsical worlds where dreams contrive.

Erratic roads in every hue,
Bananas sing, oh, how they flew!
With rubber ducks in hats of green,
They bounce and laugh, a vivid scene.

So wander through this vibrant lore,
Where dreams collide and spirits soar.
In erratic paths we find the gleam,
Of lively hearts and joyful dreams!

Wobbling Wavelengths

The sun wears stripes, oh what a sight,
As dancing waves take off in flight.
With tennis balls that float and bop,
On wobbling bands that never stop.

Silly signals, up and down,
As flamingos prance in silly gowns.
The radio plays a tune so sweet,
While swans in sunglasses tap their feet.

Curly curls all twist and shout,
In synchronized with a hula doubt.
Drawing circles, all out of line,
As laughter stretches, feeling divine.

So tune your heart to laughter's ring,
With wobbling waves that joyfully sing.
In quirky rhythms, let's engage,
For life's a dance upon the stage!

The Delight of Divergence

In the land of twisting trails,
Laughter dances in the gales.
Curves and bends, a sight so bright,
Wobble joy that feels just right.

Colors swirl, a sight to see,
Juggling shapes of jubilee.
Chasing shadows, hopping high,
Bubbling giggles race the sky.

Oddball paths weave zig and zag,
With every laugh, the woes we flag.
Lively hops and tiny leaps,
In silly dreams, the laughter sweeps.

Clouds of whimsy tickle ears,
Winding tales replace our fears.
In this circus of the fun,
We greet the rays of twinkling sun.

Fantastical Folds

In a pocket of the breeze,
Where nothing's ever what it seems,
Hats that float and shoes that dance,
Twisting fates in a merry prance.

Giggling geese and prancing mice,
Crisscross paths that look so nice.
Jumping through the loops of fate,
Every bend makes us elate.

Sunny hats of colors bright,
Spin like tops in pure delight.
When clocks march backward, time stands still,
Finding joy in zany thrill.

With every flip and silly twirl,
The world around begins to swirl.
Embrace each fold, let laughter ring,
In this madcap, joy does spring.

Loopy Legends

Once upon a time, they say,
A loop-de-loop held night and day.
With tales that twine like strings of yarn,
Every yarn spun dreams so far.

Tricky rabbits race the sun,
In circles where the fun's begun.
Dizzy hedgehogs glide and slide,
In this realm of wild joy, we bide.

Upside down and side to side,
The silliest creatures cannot hide.
From bouncing bunnies, hopping high,
To giggling clouds that drift on by.

Legends twist, they spin and swirl,
In strange dimensions, giggles whirl.
Riding on this wobbly tide,
Adventure awaits, let's glide.

Whims of Whirlwinds

When winds of whimsy start to play,
They whisk the gloom right away.
Spinning faster, twirling round,
Where laughter's lost, joy is found.

A playful breeze, a gusty sigh,
Sends hats and giggles soaring high.
Tickling trees and ticklish grass,
In a swirl, our worries pass.

Kites that loop and dance in flight,
Whirling dervishes in delight.
Chasing dreams that never tire,
In this storm, we jump higher.

Round and round, it's quite a show,
With every gust, our spirits grow.
So let the whirlwind take the lead,
And follow where the laughter's freed.

Circular Serenades

Round and round the world we go,
Dancing ducks with a witty glow.
Silly hats on frolicking heads,
Chasing cheese as laughter spreads.

Twirling trees in a wacky breeze,
Squirrels giggle, climbing with ease.
Wherever we wander, joy's in store,
Life's a circus, always wanting more.

Jumping jellies in polka-dots,
Taffy trees in candy plots.
Round and round, let's spin the tune,
Underneath a grinning moon.

In a loop, we sing our song,
Life's a merry-go, can't be wrong.
With each twist, a chuckle flows,
Round and round, now everybody knows.

Bizarre Trajectories

Flying pigs on rubber bands,
Waltzing goats in far-off lands.
On skewed paths where rabbits race,
Chasing dreams at a silly pace.

Squiggly lines draw silly frowns,
Jellybeans in trampoline towns.
Bouncing off walls, sideways we glide,
Holding on to fun with pride.

Cartwheeling cats in mismatched shoes,
Long-nosed dogs with chartreuse hues.
Everything tilts as if in jest,
Life's a puzzle; laugh is the quest.

Wobbling trails of cosmic cheer,
Through odd dimensions, we persevere.
In twists and turns, freedom is found,
On this bizarre ride, around and around.

The Art of Wandering

A wiggly line defines the path,
Where laughter reigns, and joy feels vast.
Bouncing boots in a funny jig,
Dancing shadows, oh, so big.

Clouds of cotton candy float,
Silly thoughts in a daily tote.
Skirts of daisies twirl with glee,
Whispers of whimsy in each tree.

Juggling moons and spinning suns,
Roaming freely, just for fun.
In the art of wandering, here we thrive,
Chasing quirks, feeling alive.

With a hop and a skip, we roam,
In every laugh, we find a home.
Twisted paths lead us to grace,
In the joyous rhythm of this place.

Sinuous Stories

Tales that curl like twizzler trails,
Nonsensical, full of merry gales.
Frogs in tuxedos, singing grand,
In a world that's wonderfully unplanned.

Stories twist and tumble 'round,
Where the goofy and strange abound.
Whimsical whispers, secrets blend,
In this journey, "What's next?" we send.

Loops of laughter and curves of cheer,
Never knowing what will appear.
A squiggly plot leads us to play,
In this funhouse, we'll find our way.

Scribbled fables with zigzag plots,
In every tale, a smile it knots.
Join the dance of the wild and free,
As sinuous stories create our glee.

www.ingramcontent.com/pod-product-compliance
Lightning Source LLC
Chambersburg PA
CBHW051654160426
43209CB00004B/898